Two
Principles
of
Living

Living Stream Ministry
Anaheim, CA • www.lsm.org

ISBN 978-1-57593-861-5

Living Stream Ministry
2431 W. La Palma Ave, Anaheim, CA 92801
P. O. Box 2121, Anaheim, CA 92814 USA

Printed in India

18   19   20   21   22   /   7   6   5   4   3   2

TWO PRINCIPLES
OF LIVING—
THE PRINCIPLE OF LIFE
OR
THE PRINCIPLE
OF RIGHT AND WRONG

"For we walk by faith, not by appearance" (2 Cor. 5:7).

"Behold, Moses and Elijah appeared to them, conversing with Him" (Matt. 17:3).

"When they lifted up their eyes, they saw no one except Jesus Himself alone" (v. 8).

"Hear Him!" (v. 5b).

"But to me it is a very small thing that I should be examined by you or by man's day; rather I do not even examine myself. For I am conscious of nothing against myself; but I am not justified by this, but He who examines me is the Lord" (1 Cor. 4:3-4).

"The tree of life also in the midst of the

1

garden, and the tree of knowledge of good and evil" (Gen. 2:9b).

"And the Lord God commanded the man, saying, Of every tree of the garden thou mayest freely eat: but of the tree of the knowledge of good and evil, thou shalt not eat of it: for in the day that thou eatest thereof thou shalt surely die" (vv. 16-17). (*The tree of the knowledge of good and evil can also be translated "the tree of the knowledge of right and wrong."*)

After God created man, He considered the problem of man's food. The act of giving life is the beginning of life, but food is for the maintenance of life. God created a living man and therefore needed to consider how man should live. Man should not just live; man also needs a living. God wanted man to depend on Him for his living in the same way that he was dependent upon food for his living. "For in Him we live and move and are" (Acts 17:28). Thus, God uses two trees to speak to us in a parable. The tree of life and the tree of the knowledge of good and evil are a kind of parable. They show us that man has two different kinds of food and can live either by life or by the knowledge of good and evil, that is, the knowledge of right and wrong. Many people have read about the two trees in Genesis 2, but we would like to emphasize that the two trees were put there to show us that man, especially a Christian, can live on earth according to two different principles. Man can live according to the principle of right and wrong or according to the principle of life. Some Christians take the principle of right and wrong as the standard for their living, while other Christians take the principle of life as their standard for living.

Today we would like to spend some time before God to see these two principles for living. What does it mean when a person lives according to right and wrong? What does it mean when a person lives according to life? Many people only have the tree of the knowledge of good and evil in their lives. Other people have the tree of life in their lives. Some have both trees. The Word of God tells us, however, that he who eats of the tree of the knowledge of good and evil shall surely die, while he who eats of the tree of life shall live. God also shows us that whoever lives by the knowledge of good and evil will lose his position before God. If man wants to constantly live before God, then he must know what it means to eat the fruit of the tree of life.

Two Principles of Christian Living

Here, I would like to add another principle for living: the principle of sin. You could say that everyone in the world can live according to at least three principles: they can live by sin, or they can live by right and wrong, or they can live by life.

What does this mean? It is very simple. Many people live on earth by following the lusts of their flesh. They are sons of wrath who are bound by the fashions of the world. They live and act according to the operation of the evil spirits in their hearts. Their principle for living is that they live by sin (Eph. 2:1-3). This morning I do not want to speak about this principle. I believe that many among us have already left the principle of sin. What we will consider this morning is apart from the principle of sin. These two trees represent two principles

4

of living. After becoming Christians, some people live by the principle of right and wrong, while others live by the principle of life.

In speaking about this matter, I am making the assumption that we have already left the principle of sin and are walking before God. If we would consider a little, we would see that some people live according to the principle of right and wrong or good and evil. Please remember that the principle of right and wrong, the principle of good and evil, is not Christianity. Christianity is a matter of life, not of being according to a standard. Christianity speaks of life, not of good and evil. Christianity teaches life, not right and wrong. There are many young brothers and sisters here this morning. I would like to tell you that after you received the Lord Jesus and gained a new life, you gained something marvelous inwardly. You obtained another principle of living. But if you do not know about it, you will set the principle of life aside and begin to follow the principle of right and wrong.

The Meaning of Following the Principle of Right and Wrong

What is the principle of right and wrong? If our conduct is controlled by the principle of right and wrong, then we ask if something is right or wrong whenever we have to make a decision. Would it be good to do this, or would it be evil? When we ask whether it is good, we are, in effect, asking ourselves, "Am I right to do this or not?" Many people consider much whether something is good or evil. They consider whether they can or cannot do a certain thing. They ask, "Is this right or wrong?" As they carefully consider a certain matter, being Christians, they determine whether it is good and right to do that thing. By taking care to decide whether or not something is good and right, they consider themselves to be good Christians.

God's Word says, "The tree of the knowledge of good and evil, thou shalt not eat of it: for in the day that thou eatest thereof thou shalt surely die" (Gen. 2:17). At the most, this practice is only a discerning of good from evil. At best, it is merely

6

choosing and rejecting—choosing good and rejecting evil. This is not Christianity. Christianity does not have an outward good and an outward evil. It does not have a definite standard in place. I may choose something good and reject something evil today, but this is not Christianity. It is the Old Testament, the law, worldly religions, human morality, and human ethics, but it is not Christianity.

Christianity Is Based on Life

What is Christianity? Christianity is life. Christianity is not a matter of asking whether something is right or wrong. Christianity is a matter of checking with the life inside us whenever we do something. What does the new life which God has given us tell us inwardly about this matter? It is very strange that many people have only seen an outward standard, the standard of good and evil. But God has not given us an outward standard. Christianity is not a new set of Ten Commandments. In Christianity we have not been brought to a new Sinai, nor has God given us a new set of rules and regulations with "Thou shalt" and "Thou shalt not." Christianity does not require that we ask whether something is right or wrong, good or evil. On the contrary, whenever we do anything, there is a life within us which rises up to speak with us. When we feel right inwardly, when we feel the life inside of us moving, when we are strong within and sense the anointing, we know that we have life. Many times something is right and good in the eyes of man, but strangely the inner life has no response and grows cold and retreats.

Please remember, God's Word tells us that our Christian living is based on an inner life, not an outward standard of right and wrong. Many worldly people, who are not saved, live according to the best standard of living they can attain: the principle of right and wrong. If you or I also live by the principle of right or wrong, we are the same as worldly people. Christians are different from non-Christians because we do not live by an outward standard or law. Our subject is not human morality or concepts. We do not determine whether something is right or wrong by subjecting it to human criticism or opinion. Today we have only one question: What does our inner life say? If the life is strong and active within us, we can do this; if the life is cold and retreating within us, we should not. Our principle for living is inward instead of outward. This is the only real principle of living; the others are false. People may say that many things are right to do, and I may feel that to do them is right, but what does the sense of the inner life tell us? The inner life does not agree. If we were to do them, we would not be rewarded, and if we were not to do them, there should be no shame, because they are outside of us. We can only see what is really right when the Spirit of God operates within us. If we feel that there is life inwardly, then that matter is right. If we do not feel the inward life, then the matter is wrong. Right and wrong are not decided by an outward standard but by the inner life.

The Standard of Life Is Higher Than the Standard of Good

Once this matter is resolved, we can see that we must not only avoid all that is evil but also all that is merely good. Christians

9

can only do that which comes out of life. We can see that there are evil things, good things, and things of life. We are not saying that Christians should only do things that are good and things that are of life. Rather, we are saying that Christians must not do good things or evil things. God said, "Of the tree of the knowledge of good and evil, thou shalt not eat of it: for in the day that thou eatest thereof thou shalt surely die." Note that "good and evil" are put together here as one way, while "life" is another way. Christians should not just refuse evil, they should even refuse good. There is a standard that is higher than the standard of good; it is the standard of life.

I have spoken about this matter with many young brothers, but I would like to repeat my story again today. When I first began to serve the Lord, I sought to avoid all that was evil and deliberately set myself to what was good. According to the human point of view, I seemed to be making splendid progress in avoiding evil and doing good. There was a problem, however. Since I was pursuing right and wrong,

I wanted to be clear about what was right and what was wrong in each matter before I did anything. At that time I had a co-worker who was two years older than I and we were always disagreeing. The differences that arose between us did not concern our own personal affairs. Our disagreements were about public matters, and our disputes were public too. I used to say to myself: That is wrong; if he wants to do things that way, I will protest. But no matter how much I protested, he would never give way. His only excuse was that he was two years older than I. I could argue with any other reason, but I could not argue with the fact that he was two years older than I. I could not get around this argument, but inwardly I did not agree with him. I told this story to an elderly sister, who had a wealth of spiritual experience, and I asked her to arbitrate. Was he right or was I? She did not say he was right, nor did she say he was wrong. She simply stared at me and said, "You should do as he says." I was unhappy inwardly and thought, "If I am right, tell me so; if I am wrong, then say it. Why do you say that I should do as he says?" I asked her to give me a reason for her answer. She said, "In the Lord the younger should submit to the older." "But," I retorted, "in the Lord, if the younger is right and the older wrong, must the younger still submit?" At that time I was in secondary school and had learned nothing of discipline, so I gave free vent to my anger. She still smiled and said, "You had better do as he says."

Once some people were going to be baptized, and there were three of us caring for the matter. I was the youngest, then the brother two years older than I, and finally there was a Brother Wu, who was seven years older than he. I thought, "You are two years older than I, so I have to submit to you in everything. He is even older; let us see whether or not you will submit." We got together to discuss this matter, but he refused to accept anything from Brother Wu. At every point he insisted on having his own way. Finally, he said, "Just leave things to me; I will do it alone." I thought, "What kind of logic is this? You insist that I always obey you because you are my senior, but you never need to obey your senior."

Immediately I sought out this sister to ask her about this matter. I was upset that she did not pay attention to right or wrong. She stood up and asked, "Have you not seen what the life of Christ is? Over the past few months, you have continually come to say that you are right and this brother is wrong. Do you not know what the cross is? You are insisting on the rightness of the matter, but I insist upon the life of the cross." I had been insisting upon right and wrong. I had not seen the matter of life, nor the cross. So she asked me, "Do you think you are right in doing this? Do you think you are right to say these things? Do you think it is right for you to tell me these things? They are all right according to reason, but I would ask how you feel inwardly. What is your inner sense?" I could only confess that I had been right according to reason but wrong according to the inner life.

The standard of Christian living does not only deal with evil things but also with good and right things. Many matters are right according to human standards, but the divine standard pronounces them

13

wrong because they lack the divine life. On the day to which I just referred, I saw this light for the first time. From then on I began to ask myself if the life I lived before God was according to the principle of life or the principle of what I considered right and wrong. I would check, "Am I doing this just because it is right?" The key to everything is this point: Others may say something is right. We also may say that it is right, but does the Lord's life rise up within us or does it recede when we begin to do something? When we begin to do something, do we sense the anointing or do we feel weighed down? As we are doing that thing, do we have an increasing sense that we are on the right track, or is something telling us that we are off? Please remember that life does not make decisions according to outward standards of right and wrong. Matters should be decided according to the sense of God's life or the sense of death. Decisions should be made according to God's life as it rises up or recedes within us. No Christian should say that he can do something because it is good or right. We must ask the Lord within us. What is the inner feeling that the Lord gives? Do we feel joyful inwardly about this matter? Do we have spiritual happiness and peace? These are the matters that decide our spiritual path.

When I was visiting Honor Oak, there was another brother who was also a guest there. He had many criticisms of the place. He had been a pastor and was a good preacher, and he knew that Honor Oak had much to offer spiritually. Still, he disapproved of many things. Whenever we ran into each other, he would tell me how much better his place was than Honor Oak. During the two or three months we were together, his criticism exceeded that of everyone else. One day he went too far, so I asked him, "You say Honor Oak is bad, so would it not be best if you left? Why do you remain here?" He answered, pointing to his heart, "The reason lies here; it wants to stay. Every time I pack my things to leave, my peace of heart leaves. Once I even left for two weeks, but I had to write and ask to return." I said, "Brother, have you seen these two ways: the way of life and the way of what you consider to be right or wrong?" He said, "Some days I go to my room to pack my bags as many as three times. But each time I want to leave, there is an inward forbidding. Inwardly, I feel that they are doing things wrong, but I also feel that it would be wrong for me to go." God had shown him that if he could receive spiritual help there, he should stay there to meet God. We all can see that this is not a matter of what we conceive as right or wrong. God uses His life to control His children.

Externalities Do Not Govern Decisions

The greatest error among God's children is that many people determine right and wrong by what they see. Many people determine right and wrong according to their backgrounds and based upon their years of experience. Therefore, they do not know what is really right and what is really wrong. Please remember that Christian living is based upon the inward life. Many people only have externalities before God. Many people decide what is right or wrong according to outward things. Life, however, is a different matter. Those with life know what it is.

I hope we all would see this before God: No Christian can determine anything apart from life. Whatever increases the inner life is right, and whatever decreases the inner life is wrong. No one should determine whether a matter is right or wrong by some outward standard.

I recall going to a certain place where the brothers were working with real effect. God was truly using them. If you were to ask me whether or not their work was perfect, I would have to say that there was room for improvement. In great humility they asked me to point out anything I saw that could be corrected, so I pointed out this and that. They asked me several times, but they did not change anything. Was I annoyed? No! A foolish person would become annoyed, but one who knows God could not be upset. I could only indicate external matters that needed adjustment, but I could not see what God was doing within them. I had no way to tell God what He should do within them.

In another place I visited, the brothers

were not preaching the gospel. They discussed the matter with me and asked if I thought that they should be doing so. I answered, "Doctrinally speaking, we certainly should preach the gospel." They said they realized this as well, but that surprisingly God did not give them the life to do so. Those who know God can only stand aside in silence, for our pathway is His life, not right and wrong. The difference between these two principles is immense. Brothers and sisters, the contrast here is too great. So many people only think whether it is right or wrong for them to do something. But today we should not act according to what is right and what is wrong. The one question we must ask today is whether the divine life within us rises or falls. This is what must determine the path we take. Everything is decided in our hearts.

"Hear Him"

On the Mount of Transfiguration, Moses was present, representing the outward, moral standard, and Elijah was present, representing the outward, human standard (Matt. 17:3). We all know that Moses stands

18

for the law, and Elijah stands for the prophets. The standard of the law was present, and the standard of the prophets was present. In the Old Testament the law and the prophets were most qualified to speak, but God silenced them here. God told Peter, "This is My Son, the Beloved....Hear Him!" (v. 5). Today the standard for Christian living is no longer the law, nor is it the prophets. The standard for Christian living is now Christ Himself; it is the indwelling Christ within us. Therefore, it is not a question of whether we are right or wrong but of whether or not the divine life in us agrees with something. Often, to our surprise, we find that the life within us disapproves of what we approve. When this happens, we cannot insist on what we think is right.

The Divine Life
Must Be Satisfied

I recall a story of two brothers, both Christians, who had a rice paddy. Rice paddies need to be irrigated. Their paddy was halfway up a hill; others were lower down. In the great heat of the day they drew

water and filled their paddy. In the evening
they went to sleep. But while they were
sleeping, the farmer lower down the hill
dug a hole in the irrigation channel sur-
rounding the brothers' field and let all the
water flow into his field. The next morning the brothers saw what had happened,
but they said nothing. Again they filled
the channels with water. The following day
they saw that their field had been emptied
again, but they still did not say anything.
They were Christians and felt that they
should endure in silence. This happened
every day for a week. Some people sug-
gested that they stand guard in their field
at night to catch the thief and beat him.
They did not say a word in response; they
just endured because they were Christians.

According to the human concept, they
should have been walking joyfully, happily,
and victoriously because they were enduring in silence, even after drawing water
daily and having it stolen so many times.
But strangely enough, even though they
drew water every day and remained silent
while others stole it, they did not have

peace in their hearts. They then went to see a brother with some experience in the Lord's work and said, "We do not understand why we have no peace after enduring for seven or eight days. Christians should endure and allow others to steal from them, but we do not have peace in our hearts." This brother was very experienced. He said, "You have not done enough, nor have you endured enough. You should first fill the field of the person who has stolen your water. Then you can fill your own field. Go and try this, then see whether you will have peace within." They both agreed. The next day they got up earlier than usual and filled the field of the person who had stolen their water, before filling their own field. Strangely enough, they became more and more joyful as they filled that person's field. When they came to fill their own field, they had peace in their hearts. They were at peace with the thought of allowing that person to steal their water. After two or three days of doing this, the person who had stolen their water came to apologize, saying, "If this is Christianity, I want to hear about it."

This shows us that in the realm of right and wrong, enduring is right. What more can we ask one to do? These ones had spent an entire day drawing water, and not in ordinary weather, but in hot weather. They were not educated people; they were farmers. They had done the right and good thing. What else could one ask of them? Yet they had no peace inwardly. This illustrates the way of life. This is the way we take. The way of right and wrong is another way. Man says that right is good enough, but God says that only life is sufficient. We must do things to the point that joy and peace are produced inwardly. This is the difference between the way of life and the way of right and wrong. It seems as if right and wrong are sufficient and that nothing else is needed. But God is not satisfied with being right. He requires us to satisfy the divine life.

What does the Sermon on the Mount in Matthew 5—7 teach us? It teaches us nothing less than that being right is not enough. We must do things in a way which satisfies the life God has given us. This is the content of Matthew 5—7, the Sermon on the Mount. The Sermon on the Mount does not say that everything is all right as long as things are done according to what is right. Man asks why he has to turn the other cheek when someone hits him. Is it not good enough if we do not say anything when someone strikes us? Is it not wonderful that we have not rebuked him and have shown great restraint? But God says that it is not even enough to just lower our heads and leave when we are struck. This does not satisfy the inner life. We must turn our other cheek for that person to strike as well. This means that we have no hate in our hearts. We are not angry and can endure this treatment a second time. Life is humble. Life can turn the other cheek for another blow. This is the way of life.

Many people say that Matthew 5—7 is too difficult for them. I admit that it is. It is impossible for us to carry out Matthew 5—7. If we try, we will die because we cannot do it. However, we have another life within us. It tells us that we will not be happy if we do not do this. It does not matter how much we have been offended by a brother or sister. If we do not kneel down to pray for him or her, we will not have inward joy. It is good to endure in silence, but if we do not follow the teaching of the Sermon on the Mount, we will not have inward joy. The Sermon on the Mount teaches that we must satisfy the life of God within us. In doing these things, the divine life is satisfied, released, at peace, and happy. This is the whole matter: Are we walking in the way of life or in the way of right and wrong? If we read God's Word clearly, we will see that it is wrong to decide matters by the principle of right and wrong or to live, act, and have our being according to our self-life.

There Should Be Fullness of Life Within

Sometimes we come across a brother who has acted very foolishly. According to what is proper, we should strongly exhort or rebuke him. We tell ourselves that he requires a serious, thorough dealing. We prepare ourselves to face the situation because we know he will be around for a few days. We go to his home and knock on the door, but then we ask ourselves whether we are right or wrong. He acted foolishly, so what can we do but exhort him? We have gone to his door and raised our hand to knock, but inwardly there is a problem. Our raised hand drops to our side. Even though we have convinced ourselves that we are right, this is not a matter of right or wrong. This is a matter of whether or not the life of God allows us. Many times when we go to exhort a brother, he will receive our exhortation with courtesy and promise to do what God says. Yet the more we preach to him, the more our inward being wilts. When we return home, we have to admit that we have been wrong in exhorting the brother! Therefore, it is not a matter of good or bad but a matter of being full of life inwardly.

I will give you another example. I met a needy brother a few days ago. He was extremely poor and needed some help. I thought that I certainly should do something for him because there was no prospect of help coming to him from any direction. Just at that point I had no surplus, so it was a great sacrifice to come to his aid. I seemed to be exceeding the limits of my strength to help him. According to what is proper, I was right. I should have been happy as I gave him some money. Yet for some unknown reason, I wilted inwardly as I gave him the money which I had promised to give him. A voice within said, "You are just acting on charity. That was not an act of life; it was merely human chivalry and natural kindness. It was not done in life but in yourself." God did not want me to do this. I have suffered concerning that matter for two or three weeks. Even though I had given the brother money, I had to bow before God, confess my sin, and ask His forgiveness when I reached home.

Our Living and Actions Must Be according to the Leading of Life

Brothers and sisters, as we live before God, our actions must not be determined by good and evil, but by the life within. Whatever life wants us to do is worthwhile. Anything that we do without life, no matter how good it may be, will bring us nothing but inward condemnation. A Christian should not only repent before God for the sins he has committed; often, he must repent before God for the good things he has done. The principle of our living is not one that differentiates between good and evil. We must come before God to determine what is of life and what is of death. When we have life within and feel life rising up, we are doing the proper thing. When the life does not rise up and we cannot sense the anointing in our being, we should not care whether we are acting according to right or wrong. Instead, we must confess before God and ask His forgiveness.

Paul said that he judged nothing by himself, but that only God judged him (1 Cor. 4:3-4). Many people do not understand this passage in 1 Corinthians. This sentence is very simple, but if we do not know life, it is very difficult. If we have an outward standard of good and evil, it is very easy to judge when we are wrong and right. Paul did not act according to an outward standard of right and wrong, so he could only say, "I do not even examine myself. For I am conscious of nothing against myself; but I am not justified in this, but He who examines me is the Lord." The one who examines us before the judgment seat is the Lord. In addition, we have a life within us that leads us on. That is the reason 2 Corinthians 5:7 says, "We walk by faith, not by appearance." We do not determine things by an outward, visible law. We live according to the leading which the Lord gives us inwardly.

We must learn the lesson before God that we should never act merely according to the standard of right and wrong. The standard of right and wrong is not bad; it is a good standard, but it is not good enough for a Christian. The Christian's standard surpasses right and wrong. The things which are wrong are wrong, but the things which are right are not always right. If we act according to God's life, He will show us that His demands are higher than those of human law. This being the case, it becomes very easy to live the Christian life. In every matter when we seek God's speaking within us, spontaneously there will be the shining of inward light. Please remember that our regeneration is a fact. It is also a fact that God is living in us through the Lord Jesus. The Lord is constantly expressing Himself within us. We hope that each of us would be able to say to God, "Grace me so that I live by the tree of life, not by the tree of the knowledge of good and evil. I want to constantly pay attention to life. I want to ask, 'What is the sense of life?'" If we live by this principle, we will see a great change in our Christian life.

Many problems arise because we only have a standard of right and wrong. Many mistakes are made because we do not have the standard of life. If we have the standard of life, many problems will be resolved.

Prayer

O Lord, we stand before You beseeching You to speak again. Man is empty and cannot do anything. We can only ask for Your grace to open our eyes. Every time we open our mouths or make decisions, cause us to come before You and ask if our decision is according to right and wrong or according to the inward leading of life. Lord, cause us to see the difference between what is spiritual and what is fleshly. Cause us to really see the difference between inward light and outward law. Lord, save us from the way of death. Lord, it is wrong for us to live by discerning right from wrong. May we see that discerning right from wrong is sin and death, because only those who live in death can do this. Those who live in life must be led by life. It must be the life that takes the lead. Lord, be among us so that we would see this clearly. We have said this many times, and we want to say it again: May Your Word not be spoken in vain. Cause us to know what life is and what law is. Bless these scattered utterances. Have mercy on us, and grace us. Lead us in the way before us. In the name of the Lord Jesus. Amen.